Dearly Beloved

Dearly Beloved

NAVIGATING YOUR CHURCH WEDDING

Andrew MacBeth

SEABURY BOOKS
An imprint of Church Publishing Incorporated, New York

Quotations from the marriage service in *The Book of Common
Prayer* are taken from the 1979 version.

      Library of Congress Cataloging-in-Publication Data
MacBeth, Andrew.
  Dearly beloved : navigating your church wedding /
Andrew MacBeth.
        p.   cm.
  Includes bibliographical references.
  ISBN 978-1-59627-060-2 (pbk.)
  1. Marriage—Religious aspects—Christianity. 2. Wedding
etiquette. 3. Weddings. I. Title.

BV835.M183 2007
265'.5—dc22   2007009097

Cover illustration by Charles Hefling

Printed in the United States of America

Church Publishing, Incorporated
445 Fifth Avenue
New York, New York 10016

    5   4   3   2   1

Contents

1. Introduction 1

2. Why a Wedding? 4

3. Why a Church Wedding? 7

4. Concerning the Service 15
   The Procession / *15*
   Music / *20*
   Times and Participants / *23*

5. The Shape of the Service 25
   The Exhortation and Declaration of Consent / *27*
   The Ministry of the Word / *37*
   The Marriage / *41*
   The Blessing of the Marriage / *47*
   The Eucharist / *51*
   Going Forth / *55*

6. Other Things to Think About 57
  Premarital Counseling / 57
  The Rehearsal / 59
  Photography / 62
  Superstitions and Traditions / 63
  Money Matters / 65
  Legal Matters / 68
  Honeymoons / 71
  Dealing with Family Expectations / 71
7. Unusual and Nontraditional Weddings 74
  Divorced Persons / 75
  The Role of Children / 77
  Widows and Widowers / 78
  Older Couples / 79
  Couples of Widely Different Ages / 80
  Same-sex Couples / 82
  Couples from Different Religious Traditions / 85

1

Introduction

Whether you have received this book from your pastor or picked it up on your own, its intent is the same: to help you develop some hopes and expectations about what it will mean to plan a Christian wedding with your future partner and your pastor. The book will be particularly useful to those who come from a "liturgical" tradition like my own Episcopal Church, but it will provide principles and suggestions that will be useful to other couples too.

This book will be most helpful if you read it not only before you meet with your clergy person, but before you encounter the morass that is the modern American wedding industry. It is not that the wedding industry is full of bad people (though it has its share). But it *is* an industry, smaller than automobiles but larger than steel at our last reckoning. In recent years, Americans have spent an estimated $40 to $50 billion a year on their weddings and honeymoons. To be more specific, the average wedding (without the honeymoon) now costs nearly $30,000, according to 2005 statistics. The large amount of money to be made on weddings makes it a little difficult to know who you can trust. Although I do not know your pastor, he or she is likely to be a trustworthy person with whom to plan, and an ally in dealing with the expectations of family and merchants. Here is why.

First, your pastor has probably seen a lot of weddings, large and small, in many different situations. Second, he or she is grounded in the church's tradition, which can be a great resource to you, as well as a balance to the tyranny of whatever is trendy at the moment. Finally, the pastor has little to gain from a wedding economically. (We will talk about the minister's fee, but it is seldom large enough to provide a motive for doing more weddings.) He or she may, however, hope to build a stronger relationship with you, or want to get you more involved in the life of the congregation. And a pastor may take some satisfaction in helping you plan a wedding that is both deeply Christian and truly reflective of your personal values.

If you do not have anyone in your life just yet whom you would call "your" pastor, don't worry; the process of planning for a wedding is a great way to find out if you want one and to begin such a relationship if you do. Unlike the family members and friends who have so much invested in you (and perhaps in the way they *think* you should do things), the pastor is one person who can help you sort out which of the expectations of others to meet and which ones to modify.

Whether you obtained this book from your pastor or the bookstore, reading it will equip you to take an active, knowledgeable role in planning your own wedding. Since this is something one hopes to do just once in a lifetime, most people are stuck with few reliable resources for the task—just the weddings we may have attended, the suggestions of people in the wedding industry, and the general cultural assumptions about weddings that currently reign among our friends (and perhaps our parents' friends). This is unfortunate, because there is a rich and varied tradition regarding Christian weddings. Take the time to learn a bit about this tradition in the pages that follow and you will be able to shape a wedding that is both distinctively yours *and* deeply grounded in Christian tradition.

2

Why a Wedding?

Since you are reading this book, you have probably already decided on having some kind of wedding to celebrate your marriage. Why do we do this? There are a number of reasons, even excluding such unpleasant possibilities as the desire of the couple or someone's parents to show off or hold the kind of wedding their friends or friends' children have had. One valid reason is the desire to share the beginning of a marriage with those special people who have made you who you are and who will form your support system in the months and years to come. Another is the chance to paint a picture for yourselves and your friends of the life the two of you envision sharing. A clear vision can be a powerful resource for the future. A wedding may also represent a way for members of those powerful, clingy systems we call "family" to take account of the fact that something new has happened in their web of relationships, and to begin to relate to you in new ways.

One of the things I occasionally do at a wedding is ask the couple standing at the chancel steps to turn around and look at the congregation they have assembled for this day. Ideally, it will include many of the people who have shaped their lives and actually loved them into being the individuals they are today. I may remind all those assembled that some of the bride and groom's life-shaping people are no longer living. For your wedding it is appropriate to try to gather the family members, teachers, mentors, and coworkers whose lives have had the greatest influence on you. If the number of people you can invite will be limited by the kind of reception you envision, you might want to rethink those plans. The wedding should drive your plans, not the party! (See the suggestions about receptions in chapter 6.)

Couples should also think about who will be in their support system when the wedding is over and day-to-day living begins. If your pastor does not ask you to do it in your counseling sessions, then something you should do on your own is to take a big piece of poster paper or newsprint and draw yourselves a diagram of those you expect will be vital to you and how you are connected to them. Include people from your work, church, neighborhood, and community involvements. Do not include friends from the past with whom you no longer have an active relationship. Are most of your special support people on the guest list? Some of them may not actually *know* how much you are counting on them unless you tell them. If you plan it well, your wedding can serve as a sort of commissioning for your supporters, a chance for you to acknowledge how important they are to you and a chance for them to make a commitment to give you the help you will need.

Finally, whether we recognize it or not, most of us are part of families who exercise a powerful influence on us, even years after we become independent adults. A wedding does not change this reality, but it can be a formal opportunity for family members to recognize that the constellation of relationships around you is changing. Your primary allegiance will now be to your new spouse. You will have not only your own family but your partner's to deal with now. This can be wonderful or worrisome, and it is usually a bit of both. Because planning a wedding is often stressful, the process can provide an opportunity for you to understand better the family dynamics your spouse-to-be grew up with and continues to live with today. If either of you is young or comes from a family that still tends to treat you primarily as their child, it will be especially important for you to make your own decisions in creating your wedding. Handing parents a few disappointments can help them comprehend the changes that should be underway at this point. If you cannot set your own course now, do not expect that this will change when you get back from your honeymoon.

To be honest, most people do not really plan their own wedding. They simply reproduce, with minor variations, the weddings they have seen friends or family members have. Many couples have sadly realized, even before the day of the wedding, that they have ended up with a wedding that does not really reflect their values and their vision. Often the disconnect has to do with spending money in ways they cannot justify, despite the fact that there is clearly no correlation between the cost of a wedding and the future happiness of the couple. A wedding *should* be a real celebration, but where does a good party end and excess begin? You can talk with your pastor not just about the marriage you envision and the wedding service at which he or she will preside but about the whole wedding process. Together, you can strategize about how to make your wedding an event that truly represents your best values and your hopes for the future.

3

Why a Church Wedding?

*I*n most western nations today, having a church wedding requires a much clearer choice than it does for Americans. In these other countries, marriages are legally complete when one leaves the government office that records them. Only in the United States are clergy routinely licensed to perform marriages in the name of the state, a considerable irony given our highly valued tradition of separation between church and state. Exactly how this works varies from state to state, but in most cases, when a couple goes to the local government office where marriages are recorded and fills out the paperwork there, what they are doing is indicating an *intention* to marry. The marriage will be recorded as complete only when a minister, magistrate, or some person who is licensed to oversee the exchange of marriage promises certifies that the couple has actually made them. In most of the United States, therefore, the assumption is made that *some* sort of ceremony beyond what happens at the marriage license office will probably take place. This may just happen in the office of the marriage commissioner down the hall, but it is more likely to happen in a church or a church-like setting, no matter what the religious sensibilities of the couple may be.

For this reason, a church with an attractive sanctuary will have people coming to the door from time to time who assume that making arrangements for using the church building should be like any other part of their preparations—a matter of scheduling, cost, and groundrules. If one or both of you are serious Christians, however, your reasons for choosing to have your wedding in the church may be different.

The most obvious reason for having your wedding in a church is that the building is a tangible symbol of God's presence. Of course, Christians believe God is present everywhere. But churches are specifically designed to be a visible sign for us of God's presence, to help us tune in to the fact (of which we may not always be aware) that God *is* there. For Christians and for Jews, there is a strong tradition suggesting God cares that commitments between people are made and kept, particularly marriage commitments. A number of the Ten Commandments involve the commitments of marriage and family, and not only the one that says, "Thou shalt not commit adultery." Although Jesus does not seem to have been married, at least one glimpse we get of Jesus' life involves his participation in a wedding in the village of Cana, and quite a number of the parables that Jesus told display an intimate familiarity with the way weddings were celebrated in his own time.

What specifically *is* God's stake in the marriage of two Christians? At baptism, we say that each disciple of Christ is given unique gifts, gifts that are intended to be used by that person to carry out the specific task or "ministry" to which

God has called them. Given our theology of vocation, most Christians would say that God's call to each of the individual partners in a marriage has to be respected and, hopefully, advanced by their new call to marry. It may also be that the couple can accomplish things for God together that would be unlikely for them to do individually.

Whether your pastor is open to performing a wedding in some setting outside the church building is a question you can explore with him or her, if you have a reason for doing this. Perhaps the reception is going to be held at a remote location, such as a family ranch, which is a long way from the nearest church. In practice, I have found that many couples who want a Christian minister involved but do not want the wedding itself held in a church are avoiding something. Most often, that "something" is the question of the couple's own religious commitments. Perhaps the groom is far more deeply religious than the bride. Or perhaps the bride's family is so devoutly Roman Catholic that the couple, who don't want to get married in the Catholic Church, think it will be less of an issue if they do not get married in a church at all. Whatever the situation, if this sort of religious confusion applies to you, it is worthwhile trying to sort out some of the questions before you plan the details of your wedding.

If the question of just how much "church" you want in your lives is an issue for one or both of you, you will find that most clergy will understand your questioning about faith and the church, and you may be able to find a pastor who will be helpful in working it out. Let me share what my own congregation says to couples who are wondering about whether or not they want to be married in our church—or any church!

Should Your Wedding Be a Church Wedding?

Holding your wedding in a church makes a faith statement. Be sure it is the statement you want to make. People who are planning to marry find themselves in at least three different places with regard to the Christian church:

1. Some people have found that being part of a community of faithful Christians gives shape and meaning to their lives. Without the church, its fellowship and worship life, it would be hard for them to be the people they believe they are called to be. They have made a commitment, as our Book of Common Prayer puts it, "to work, pray, and give for the spread of the Kingdom of God" through their participation in a specific Christian congregation.

2. Some people have a personal relationship with God that they find needs no support from an institution like the church. This does not mean, however, that they do not want God's help and blessing for their marriage. Many young Americans would put themselves in this category.

3. Some people are not sure. Maybe they do want and need to be part of a community of people who come together to seek God's will for their lives—and maybe not. It may be that they have been getting along without much visible connection to the church for some time. Getting married, however, raises all sorts of questions. Sometimes, the future bride or groom—or both—will have a sense that perhaps a relationship with Christ and his church is something they want and need.

We believe the church is involved with weddings primarily because people in Category #1 above want to make their marriage commitment within the community that already gives shape and meaning to their lives. The church invests the time, care, and energy of its members (and the use of its facilities) to support couples in living out the challenging covenant of marriage—both now and in the years ahead.

If you find yourselves in Category #3 above, you will find that many congregations will be interested in working with you to explore both your marriage commitment and the meaning of Christian community. To do this, your wedding date needs to be far enough in the future that you can share actively in the church's worship and small group life for some time before the wedding. In our experience, it takes six months or so to really become a part of a congregation. If you commit to expend the effort to really get involved in the life of a church—and really follow through on this undertaking—we think the church should commit to hold your wedding, whether or not you ultimately decide to be baptized or confirmed or otherwise commit to long-term membership. If you make such an investment in exploring life within a faith community, you can be pretty confident that when your wedding day comes, you will feel fully at home in the place where you will be married and among these people who have agreed to support you.

If you find yourselves in Category #2, believing that your relationship with God is a private matter that for the most part needs no institutional or communal expression, try to be consistent as you plan your wedding. Consider having your ceremony in the place where you will hold the reception. There are clergy and marriage commissioners in the community who will do their best to give your wedding a spiritual dimension. There may also be churches in your community that will make their sanctuary available for your service for a fee, with relatively few strings attached. You have to be sure, of course, that having your wedding in a church will feel right to you, especially if church membership does not.

There may be a Category #4. If the two of you find yourselves in radically different places with regard to religious faith, you have a serious challenge ahead. If the one of you who is least inclined to feel the need of a relationship with the visible church honestly believes you can support your partner in his or her living out a church relationship, there is biblical precedent for the church supporting your wedding. Be aware, however, that couples tend to underestimate the challenges involved in having to share their spouse with a faith community they do not particularly care about. Being a serious Christian involves some sacrifices and certainly affects people's major life decisions. Just as you would need to take seriously the consequences of your spouse-to-be being a Navy SEAL, a rock musician, or an orthopedic surgeon, now is the time to find out about the ways your beloved's life will be shaped by his or her faith commitment. Is she really going to spend two hours each week in church? Does he expect to tithe his income to church and charity?

Here are some other questions we are frequently asked:

What about marrying people who do not live in the area?
When people who live out of town need to be married in our community for some reason, they can be married in our church if our schedule permits and if one or both of the couple are active communicants of an Episcopal parish where they live. Our expectation is that they will receive premarital counseling through their home parish. A fee is charged for such weddings to help cover the costs to this congregation.

What about being married in the church of our parents?
In this parish, children of active, communicant members of our parish are expected to be active members of this—or some other—local church *or* to share actively in our worship and parish life for six months or more before the wedding—just like anybody else! Children who live outside the local area are expected to have—or to establish—a church relationship in the place where they live during the period before

the wedding and to receive premarital counseling through that church.

What about people who have been previously married and divorced?
In our Episcopal Church tradition, divorced persons may marry in the church, but only after special counseling and with the consent of our local bishop. If this is your situation, be sure to let your pastor know right away. Requiring the bishop's permission for remarriage is the church's way of trying to maintain its vision of marriage as a lifelong union while still being able to support previously married people, when appropriate, in making and living out a new commitment.

The process of obtaining the bishop's permission is in some ways just the opposite of what has been called an "annulment." That is, rather than seeking a rationale for declaring that a valid marriage never existed, it forces us to acknowledge the reality of the previous marriage and come to terms with it. There are a number of questions to be answered, but a minister of our church might *decline* to marry you if he or she felt that:

- the marriage might interfere with the care of your children;
- some of the issues that caused the break-up of your first marriage are still unresolved;
- you have not established sufficient connection with the church for your pastor to get involved in the first place.

We are Roman Catholic (or members of some other denomination) and we do not want to go through our church's marriage or remarriage procedures. Can you help us?
We believe strongly that couples should follow the disciplines of their own denomination, so we do not hold weddings for Catholics or others who want to avoid dealing with their own church's expectations and discipline. People who are ready to explore joining our denomination, however, are welcome to do so.

Getting Involved

If you are not already involved in the church, do not fear. You may find that some clergy are a bit reluctant to talk about weddings with people they have never seen. It makes a huge difference to us if the couple has actually come to church together once or twice to check us out. Believe it or not, clergy are often frustrated with couples who do not seem to take the planning of the wedding service as seriously as we do. A little theological seriousness on your part will be greatly appreciated by whoever meets with you about your hopes and plans for your wedding and your life together. Let the pastor know you have been reading and talking together about marriage. He or she will be impressed!

What if you come from different religious traditions? There are whole books on this subject. As with any other couple, however, the willingness of your faith communities to get involved will depend greatly on whether or not you have an active relationship with them. In my own experience, it has proven easier to work with a couple where both have a strong religious commitment, however different, than in a situation where either the bride or the groom is just religious enough to want to do things in his or her own way. Most clergy will be more than willing to invest the extra time and effort required to help craft a wedding ceremony that respects both of your faith traditions—if you will do the same.

4

Concerning the Service

THE PROCESSION

More energy gets spent on how the wedding party enters the church than on the whole rest of the service! This is probably unfortunate, but it's not likely to change anytime soon. The procession matters because it sets the tone for the rest of the wedding and helps tell the congregation what sort of event this is. Let's look at some of the ways that the formal "gathering" of the wedding party can be carried out—and what they signify.

What many of us think of as the "traditional" wedding procession dates back only to the late Victorian age. Being able to mount an elaborate procession meant that a family had, or aspired to, a certain social status. There are glaring problems with repeating this kind of procession today. Having the bride and groom enter the church from different directions symbolizes suspicion, not unity. Your wedding is not a confrontation between the Hatfields and McCoys; it is a gathering of those who love you, united in support.

Another element of "traditional" processions—placing a veiled bride at the end of a long line of bridesmaids—does give the bride a certain importance, but it also turns her into an object for evaluation. The custom of veiling the bride and not letting the groom see her on the wedding day is a throwback to the days of arranged marriages, when the bride and groom really might not know who they were marrying until they met at the altar.

In some places it is still the custom for the bride's father to stand between the bride and groom for the first part of the service, another symbol of suspicion. Under this scenario, the father only takes his seat after the Declaration of Consent—that is, after the groom has declared his intentions to be honorable. Passing the hand of a woman who cannot see where she is going from one male to another suggests that she is a helpless creature who needs custodial care. Asking the question, "Who gives this woman to be married to this man?" makes it official. The Episcopal Book of Common Prayer has discouraged this practice since 1976, though some couples who wish to include it in the service soften the patriarchal imagery by having the parents of both the bride and the groom "give away" their children.

In summary, the statements that these "traditional" elements of the service make may not be what the couple intend when they say they want a "traditional" service. More likely, the call for tradition is a plea for a service that touches the heart, sounds an appropriate note of solemnity, and represents a genuine celebration.

Some couples want to cut down on the pomp and circumstance involved in a wedding, for a variety of reasons. I happen to think that older couples and folks who have had previous marriages should celebrate just as lavishly as younger couples. However, if simplicity is your goal, one of the best ways to achieve it is by eliminating the procession. Just have the bride and groom take seats in the front row of the church's seating area ten minutes or so before the wedding. Relax and enjoy the music (you *are* having music, aren't you?) until it is time for the service to begin.

If you choose to have a procession, think for a moment about the purpose of a procession in the marriage service, and what you want it to signify. First, it should help get people into a "worship" mindset, with a sense that they have come to *take part* in a worship service and offer their hearts and minds to a celebration of this bride and groom's life together. Those who are unfamiliar with church services may come with the rather unfortunate notion that they have come to sit back and *watch* a wedding, a sort of a marriage pageant. The procession should be a way to signify that each person is an important and active participant in the service. Second, the procession should convey a sense of unity: whatever our differences of culture or status may be, this is a time to set those things aside. Finally, the procession can be a way to introduce the principal participants in the wedding: here is the bride, the groom, the minister, (perhaps) the parents, and others.

If you belong to a faith tradition in which worship services frequently begin with a procession, make your wedding procession as much as possible like the one you have on Sunday morning. For Episcopalians, this means that the procession will be led by the processional cross. (Your pastor will not have any trouble recruiting a young person to carry it. Or there may be a family member or friend who can do it or who could be trained specially for this occasion.) It is customary to stand when the cross comes in. Whether the procession is led by the cross or not, instruction can be given at the rehearsal that the congregation is meant to stand up immediately when the procession begins.

The clergy and any other ancillary ministers, such as chalice bearers for communion, will follow the cross. They will normally be vested in white or the color of the most festive vestments your church has. They are followed by the groom and best man (unless the groom is walking beside the bride—see below).

You have choices about how the bridesmaids and groomsmen enter. The men can enter two by two behind the ministers and the groom, followed by the women, one at a time. I refer to this as the "Atlantic City" option, because it has distinct similarities to a beauty pageant or to fashion models on the runway. Despite this jibe, a lot of time and attention may have gone into the women's dresses, flowers, and so on, so if the Atlantic City option seems like *fun* to you, by all means do it. On the other hand, plenty of brides and bridesmaids hate the idea of a solo trip down the aisle, either because they feel it objectifies them or simply because they think having all eyes on them is going to make them nervous.

Another option is to have the bridesmaids and groomsmen come down the aisle in couples. Men and women will probably separate as they approach the altar, in order to stand in support behind the bride or groom. Recently, I have had occasional queries from brides and grooms about what to do with the best friend who happens to be of the opposite sex. I predict that more and more weddings will feature a mixture of male and female witnesses at each side of the altar.

At the rehearsal, ask members of the procession to walk at a dignified pace suitable to the solemnity of the occasion. Don't let them do a hesitation step, however, or try to keep their steps in unison. This tends to get the couple swaying back and forth like sailor-buddies coming out of a pier-side bar.

Having children in the procession can be fun for all concerned, but please do not ask really young children to serve as ring-bearers or flower-bearers, cute as two- and three-year-olds can be. It is impossible to predict how very young children will react to the attention of so many people. Even more important is the question of how the experience will be for them. If there are children involved in your procession, make sure they receive careful guidance at the rehearsal and consider providing them a place to sit with their family members after they have made the walk down the aisle.

Who brings up the rear, the supposed place of honor in the procession? If I had my way, it would be the bride alone or the bride and groom together. Another option is to have all the parents in the procession, the groom's parents with him and the bride's parents with her. This is a good way to dramatize their support and the important role that both mothers and fathers may have had in bringing their children to maturity.

I have had my best luck getting people to accept one of these suggestions when the bride's father is not available to walk with her. If I had a daughter (and I don't—only sons), I think I would be even more proud to watch her come down the aisle on her own than with her hand on my steadying arm. This said, it may be exactly right for the bride's father to escort his daughter to the altar in your wedding. It really is true that fathers have a powerful influence on their daughters' sense of self and their daughters' expectations about the respect they should receive from a future husband.

Unless the bride and groom have come down the aisle together, the bride's escort(s) places her hand in the groom's, then takes a seat. If the bride intends to wear a veil that is actually down over her face (though she should ask herself, why would I do this?), this is the moment to turn it back. The father or other escort can help. You cannot contract a marriage with someone whose eyes you cannot see!

MUSIC

In most weddings, music is essential and sets the tone for the celebration. If you and your church's musician work together, you can shape the atmosphere of the service right from the prelude. Ask that the musician select only music that might be played before a worship service on Sunday morning. This means you probably will not have to endure excerpts from opera or syrupy hymns to love, and it means that by the time the service begins and without anyone saying a word, members of the congregation will find themselves expecting to be part of a worship service, not just spectators at a wedding. Music for the procession can be full of pomp and circumstance, as at a graduation ceremony (or a coronation!), or it can be more pastoral, or more festive and energetic. Be sure to let your church musician play you a number of different selections before you choose.

You might consider beginning the service with the singing of a hymn, though because people in the congregation are more inclined to watch the procession than sing, it is a good idea to start singing only after the wedding party is in place. Like the prayers of the wedding service, the words of the hymns used in weddings contain rich and meaningful theology that too often passes us by in the course of the service. In considering possible hymns for your wedding, read them aloud together as a couple and see what they say to you.

♫ Hymns for Weddings

The following hymns that are appropriate for weddings are found in the Episcopal Church's *Hymnal 1982*. The hymnals of other denominations likewise have a number of suitable hymns. One important consideration when selecting hymns, however, is how familiar the hymn tune will be to the congregation. If one of your favorites is a hymn no one else will know, you might want to reconsider your choice or have the choir sing the hymn as an anthem. If you want a soloist to sing, one of the blessing hymns might be a good choice; talk with your pastor about where it would fit best in the service.

Opening Hymns and Hymns of Praise
- Give praise and glory unto God (375)
- Joyful, joyful, we adore thee, God of glory, Lord of love (376)
- God is Love, let heaven adore him; God is Love, let earth rejoice (379)
- Praise to the Lord, the Almighty, the King of creation (390)

Hymns of Thanksgiving
- Praise to God, immortal praise, for the love that crowns our days (288)
- Now thank we all our God, with heart, and hands, and voices (397)
- For the beauty of the earth, for the beauty of the skies (416)
- For the fruit of all creation, thanks be to God (424)

Metrical Settings of the Psalms
- Praise to the Lord, the Almighty, the King of creation (390; Psalm 103)
- God of mercy, God of grace, show the brightness of thy face (538; Psalm 67)
- The King of love my shepherd is (645; Psalm 23)
- My shepherd will supply my need, Jehovah is his Name (664; Psalm 23)

Before the Gospel
- Lord of all hopefulness, Lord of all joy (482)
- Be thou my vision, O Lord of my heart (488)
- Spirit divine, attend our prayers, and make this house thy home (509)

Hymns While Setting the Communion Table
- Father, we thank thee who hast planted thy holy Name within our hearts (302 and 303)
- I come with joy to meet my Lord, forgiven, loved, and free (304)
- Lord, we have come at your own invitation, chosen by you, to be counted as friends (348)
- God is love, and where true love is God himself is there (577)

Blessing Hymns
- May the grace of Christ our Savior... rest upon them from above (351)
- O God, to those who here profess their vows of life-long love (352)
- Your love, O God, has called us here, for all love finds its source in you (353)
- O Jesus, joy of loving hearts, the fount of life and our true light (649)

Communion Hymns
- Let us break bread together on our knees (325)
- Come with us, O blessed Jesus, with us evermore to be (336)
- For the bread which you have broken, for the wine which you have poured (341)
- Seek ye first the kingdom of God and its righteousness (711)

Closing Hymns
- ❧ Go forth for God; go to the world in peace (347)
- ❧ Joyful, joyful, we adore thee, God of glory, Lord of love (376)
- ❧ Love divine, all loves excelling, joy of heaven, to earth come down (657)
- ❧ All my hope on God is founded; he doth still my trust renew (665; especially verses 1, 4, 5)

TIMES AND PARTICIPANTS

Consult with the minister who will preside about when to schedule your wedding, and how much time to allow for pre-service preparations, the wedding, after-service photos, and travel to the reception. Once you have set a time for the wedding, stick to it and be prepared to *start your wedding on time!* This may be "your day," but it is still rude for a bride or groom to keep guests waiting. It is ruder still for parents to do this, so let them know you expect them to be on time because you would hate for them to miss anything.

My experience with wedding bulletins or programs is that they are most useful as a way to list service participants so that the guests at your wedding can figure out who is who. They do not help the congregation much in following the service unless you print out every word, maybe including even the lessons and hymns. Such a multi-page booklet is a lot of work but it does eliminate the need for the minister to announce every page number. Or you may decide you will not need any bulletin at all.

If you decide you want some sort of bulletin, your printing options include: a single sheet that lists the participants and perhaps the starting page number in the Prayer Book; a bulletin containing lots of page and hymn numbers (much like the typical Sunday service bulletin); or a full text of the service. Your church can probably provide examples from previous weddings, and your pastor will certainly want to look over your draft before you go to press. Some churches will even print bulletins for you, but do not be surprised if they suggest you just take them to a printer for copying.

5

The Shape of the Service

*G*iven my Episcopal liturgical tradition, I would say that what makes a wedding "Christian" is two Christian people *and* a congregation—and a congregation is *not* the same as an audience! As we examine the shape of the wedding service as it is celebrated in the 1979 Book of Common Prayer, we will make a point of discovering the things that invite the congregation to be active participants in the wedding and those that turn them into mere observers (which I believe ought to be avoided).

The marriage service contains beautiful and meaningful prayers for couples that are too easily overlooked in the stress of the wedding ceremony. Why not pray them together in the weeks before the marriage takes place, talk them over, or commit them to memory? You will find such prayers a

The Celebration and Blessing of a Marriage

At the time appointed, the persons to be married, with their witnesses, assemble in the church or some other appropriate place.

During their entrance, a hymn, psalm, or anthem may be sung, or instrumental music may be played.

Then the Celebrant, facing the people and the persons to be married, with the woman to the right and the man to the left, addresses the congregation and says

Dearly beloved: We have come together in the presence of God to witness and bless the joining together of this man and this woman in Holy Matrimony. The bond and covenant of marriage was established by God in creation, and our Lord Jesus Christ adorned this manner of life by his presence and first miracle at a wedding in Cana of Galilee. It signifies to us the mystery of the union between Christ and his Church, and Holy Scripture commends it to be honored among all people.

The union of husband and wife in heart, body, and mind is intended by God for their mutual joy; for the help and comfort given one another in prosperity and adversity; and, when it is God's will, for the procreation of children and their nurture in the knowledge and love of the Lord. Therefore marriage is not to be entered into unadvisedly or lightly, but reverently, deliberately, and in accordance with the purposes for which it was instituted by God.

rich resource that will help you to navigate the wedding itself and be a source of strength and companionship in the months and years ahead.

THE EXHORTATION AND DECLARATION OF CONSENT

The service usually begins with an exhortation or address by the presider that explains why we are together. In the Book of Common Prayer, we hear that we have gathered in the presence of God "to witness and bless" the joining together of bride and groom. To be witness to an auto accident is a matter of pure happenstance, but to be invited to serve as a witness to someone's marriage vows is a weighty matter. Conversely, for the couple, making vows in front of *these* particular people invests the promises with the highest possible gravity. A bride and groom's witnesses are the people whose support they believe will be most vital to the success of their marriage. We might call them the "guarantors," people who are committed to the bride and groom and their life as wife and husband.

If you are young enough that parents will have an important role in the planning of your wedding, talk to them about who should be there. There is nothing terribly wrong with inviting people because they do business with your parents or because they are your parents' friends, but make sure that the first people on your list are the ones whose support you believe you actually will need in the years ahead.

Given all that has just been said, one of your goals for planning your wedding must be to see that your "guarantors" have every opportunity to actually participate in the service and make a commitment of their own to support and uphold you in your marriage.

If Banns are to be published, the following form is used

I publish the Banns of Marriage between N. N. of _____ and N. N. of _____ . If any of you know just cause why they may not be joined together in Holy Matrimony, you are bidden to declare it. This is the first (or second, or third) time of asking.

In addition to witnessing, we say that we have come to "bless" the couple's union. Christians and Jews believe that God has a stake in the commitments human beings make to one another. I do not believe that God cares more about believers than unbelievers, but I *do* believe that our awareness of God's loving care helps us be receptive to it. There is power in the solemn and public announcement of our belief that *God cares*. God has a stake in human relationships and recognizing this is indeed a great blessing. Also, Jesus made the bold claim that God has a special investment in the lives of people who are willing to be instruments of God's love in the world. If two such persons marry, surely God is present in the front row, along with the witnesses.

The Exhortation tells us that there are three purposes of marriage: the couple's "mutual joy; the help and comfort given one another in prosperity and adversity; and, when it is God's will, the procreation of children and their nurture in the knowledge and love of the Lord." I hope the next edition of the Prayer Book will modify that third clause to suggest that there are many ways in which a couple may possibly be called to "bear fruit" for God and God's kingdom, and that raising faith-filled children is only one of them. If you and your pastor want to experiment with a change and share the results with your diocesan liturgical commission, I suggest something like this: "and to enhance their ability to serve as ministers of Christ and heralds of his kingdom."

The Exhortation ends with the one opportunity in the service for the full names of the bride and the groom to be read aloud: "Into this holy union *N. N.* and *N. N.* now come to be joined." Even if you have four long and difficult names, they should all be read here. Be sure the minister practices saying them at the rehearsal. Names can be tricky.

✆ *The Banns*

Everything that happens before the reading of the lessons was historically part of one or more preliminary rites that

The Celebrant, facing the people and the persons to be married, with the woman to the right and the man to the left, addresses the congregation and says

Into this holy union N. N. and N. N. now come to be joined. If any of you can show just cause why they may not lawfully be married, speak now; or else for ever hold your peace.

Then the Celebrant says to the persons to be married

I require and charge you both, here in the presence of God, that if either of you know any reason why you may not be united in marriage lawfully, and in accordance with God's Word, you do now confess it.

took place weeks or months before the actual solemnizing of the marriage. The celebrant's request to the congregation that "if any of you can show just cause why they may not be lawfully married, speak now; or else for ever hold your peace" is definitely a holdover from the days when the "banns of marriage" were published at least three times in the weeks before a wedding so that anyone who knew that one of the couple already had a spouse and children in another county could speak up. Today, the question is for the most part a silly bit of drama, but if it is going to be read, it deserves to be followed with an ominous pause. I have never had anyone speak up during this time except for one unhappy mother of the groom, and since that difficult and combative lady made her pronouncements on her son and his intended many years ago, I have mentioned at the rehearsal that no one should say a peep at this point unless they have in their possession documents testifying to a genuine legal impediment to the marriage.

The question to the couple as to whether *they* know any reason why they may not lawfully be married probably needs changing in the next edition of the Prayer Book. It would be good if we could state at this point that the bride and groom have carefully examined their motives for marriage and believe them to be wholesome. There are unlikely to be any undisclosed legal impediments to your marriage, but there could be some factors that inhibit the making of a free and healthy commitment.

If there are certain reservations or secrets that you bring to your coming marriage, use the pre-marriage period and the counseling you will do together then to bring these things to the surface. If you fathered a child when you were sixteen, it would be good to tell that story now, rather than simply hoping your child does not come knocking on your door someday in an effort to discover more about his origins. If your promises contain any reservations, please discuss them with your minister as well as your spouse-to-be.

The Declaration of Consent

The Celebrant says to the woman

N., will you have this man to be your husband; to live together in the covenant of marriage? Will you love him, comfort him, honor and keep him, in sickness and in health; and, forsaking all others, be faithful to him as long as you both shall live?

The Woman answers

I will.

The Celebrant says to the man

N., will you have this woman to be your wife; to live together in the covenant of marriage? Will you love her, comfort her, honor and keep her, in sickness and in health; and, forsaking all others, be faithful to her as long as you both shall live?

The Man answers

I will.

The Prayer Book wedding vows are sweeping and allow little room for holding anything back. Some examples might be that, although you are of childbearing age, you know that having children is not an option. Another might be your awareness that living in something less than a sixteen-room house would be more than you could bear. Or perhaps moving more than an hour's drive from your family would be completely out of the question. Your pastor can help the two of you sort through what reservations, if any, are compatible with the vows you are about to make. (See the section in chapter 6 on prenuptial agreements.)

🦋 The Declaration of Consent

The Declaration of Consent is important because of what it says about the nature of the commitment that the man and the woman are making. The marriage commitment is described not as a contract, in which one person agrees to do something in exchange for the other party's promise to do or give something in return, but as a *covenant*. This is the same word Holy Scripture uses to describe the relationship between God and human beings. God's covenant with us does not depend on the hope of receiving a human response, frail and inconsistent as our response may be. On the contrary, it is an expression of the divine nature itself. God is described in Scripture as one who loves us freely, simply because God chooses to love. There is no hint in the election of Israel or the calling of Jesus' disciples that God has chosen these particular people because they are the best around. Neither does God stop loving us when we fail the relationship in some important way. God may register disappointment, but we are not rejected; we are still God's people.

In the same way, in the covenant of marriage, two people pledge not just to love one another until they experience some disappointment with their partner, but to love as long as the other will let them, without regard to the other's merit—just as God loves us. One could say that the covenant

The Celebrant then addresses the congregation, saying

Will all of you witnessing these promises do all in your power to uphold these two persons in their marriage?

People   We will.

If there is to be a presentation or a giving in marriage, it takes place at this time.

A hymn, psalm, or anthem may follow.

of marriage is more than a "fifty-fifty" proposition; it is "hundred-hundred," based on an unconditional commitment from both sides. In God's case, and perhaps even in ours, we might say that it is a commitment based on the character of the lover, not the worthiness of the beloved.

Notice that the questions in the Declaration of Consent begin with the words "Will you...," with the expected response, "I will." This promise of future behavior stands in marked contrast to the words often heard in television weddings: "I do." This is because our bride and groom are not being asked to state their present attitude toward their partner, as in "Do you think he looks good all dressed up in his tuxedo?" (Answer: "I do.") Rather, they are being asked to make a covenant. Again, a covenant is quite different from a contract, because in a contract there is a built-in reciprocity. I agree to bear your children, keep your house, and have supper on the table at six each night, and you agree in exchange to provide a certain level of household income, mow the lawn, and so on. If you fail to perform all your agreed functions, then I will be completely justified in shirking some of my duties, too. We can get into a vicious circle in which each of us pulls things off the table until we get to the point at which there is no more contract left. In a covenant, on the other hand, the parties state what they intend to do and what sort of response they are hoping for, but it is clear that their continued performance of their commitment has more to do with their own character than their partner's performance.

One might say that a new community is being formed in the uniting of this man and woman. They are a mini-church, united (like the people gathered around them) by a decision to love. This explains how it is possible for the presider to ask, "Will you love him..." and so forth. We cannot promise to always have loving feelings toward our neighbor or our spouse, but we *can* promise to behave lovingly and to

The Ministry of the Word

The Celebrant then says to the people

The Lord be with you.

People   And also with you.

Let us pray.

O gracious and everliving God, you have created us male and female in your image: Look mercifully upon this man and this woman who come to you seeking your blessing, and assist them with your grace, that with true fidelity and steadfast love they may honor and keep the promises and vows they make; through Jesus Christ our Savior, who lives and reigns with you in the unity of the Holy Spirit, one God, for ever and ever. *Amen.*

Then one or more of the following passages from Holy Scripture is read. If there is to be a Communion, a passage from the Gospel always concludes the Readings.

Genesis 1:26–28 (Male and female he created them)
Genesis 2:4–9, 15–24 (A man cleaves to his wife
    and they become one flesh)
Song of Solomon 2:10–13; 8:6–7 (Many waters
    cannot quench love)
Tobit 8:5b–8 *(New English Bible)* (That she and I
    may grow old together)

1 Corinthians 13:1–13 (Love is patient and kind)
Ephesians 3:14–19 (The Father from whom every
    family is named)
Ephesians 5:1–2, 21–33 (Walk in love, as Christ
    loved us)
Colossians 3:12–17 (Love which binds everything
    together in harmony)
1 John 4:7–16 (Let us love one another for love
    is of God)

treat one another with love, even on the days when we do not feel especially loving.

A welcome innovation in the 1979 Book of Common Prayer is the provision for a question to the congregation: "Will you who witness these vows do all in your power to uphold these two persons in their marriage?" At minimum, members of the congregation should respond with a vociferous, "We will." If you want to encourage hooting or clapping, go right ahead, but be aware that since in many places people are still socialized to be silent in church, the response needs to be practiced at the rehearsal. Most of the time, when ministers ask a question of their congregation in church, they are not really expecting a response! This question emphasizes the opportunity for your guests to join you in your commitment. In the upcoming homily, the preacher may want to make some concrete suggestions about ways that those present can carry out the support they have promised to give. I believe this includes giving you the space to be yourselves, but also being present for you when needed.

THE MINISTRY OF THE WORD

After the singing of a hymn, the collect signals that we are clear about why we have gathered and that we are ready to hear God's word in Holy Scripture. The Prayer Book collect is rather prosaic; I suggest you consider writing a collect of your own with your pastor's help. What is it that you most need to ask for on your wedding day? Models of prayers may be found in the Prayer Books of other churches in the Anglican Communion, as well as in the worship books from other denominations.

After the prayer, the congregation is (finally!) seated. We have come to the heart of the service, our time to listen to

Between the Readings, a Psalm, hymn, or anthem may be sung or said. Appropriate Psalms are 67, 127, and 128.

When a passage from the Gospel is to be read, all stand, and the Deacon or Minister appointed says

> The Holy Gospel of our Lord Jesus Christ according to _____ .

People   Glory to you, Lord Christ.

Matthew 5:1–10 (The Beatitudes)
Matthew 5:13–16 (You are the light . . . Let your light so shine)
Matthew 7:21, 24–29 (Like a wise man who built his house upon the rock)
Mark 10:6–9, 13–16 (They are no longer two but one)
John 15:9–12 (Love one another as I have loved you)

After the Gospel, the Reader says

> The Gospel of the Lord.

People   Praise to you, Lord Christ.

A homily or other response to the Readings may follow.

God's word to us. You might think the Bible would be full of teaching about marriage, but it is not, at least not directly. What we *do* find in the Scriptures is all kinds of wisdom and challenge regarding human relationships, commitment, and our calling to love and serve one another. Seating can be provided for the wedding party too, but, in my experience, couples seldom elect to sit, even in churches where this is practicable. Think it over—you may listen better if you are seated.

The two or three Scripture readings will normally include an Old Testament lesson, a reading from the Epistles, and a Gospel reading. If the wedding will be a Eucharist (that is, will include Holy Communion), one of the readings *must* be from the Gospels. The bride and groom should choose the readings. The list from the Book of Common Prayer is a good place to begin, but there are other lists worth consulting. If you listen to the Scriptures regularly during the months of your engagement, either at worship or in your own daily devotions, you are likely to hear a number of lessons that help you comprehend God's call to you in marriage. Keep track of these readings in your wedding notebook and consider them when it comes time to choose. Occasionally, a reading from a secular source is added. Although it made me nervous when a couple told me recently that they wanted a passage from *Jane Eyre* read at their wedding, they paired it with a challenging passage from the letter to the Ephesians, and together these readings made a powerful faith statement.

The Homily

It will be helpful if you tell your pastor *why* you have chosen the particular readings you have, because the next thing that happens in your service should be a very brief homily (a mini-sermon) that points out the connections between the readings you have chosen and the marriage commitment you are making. Make sure the person entrusted with giving the

39

The Marriage

The Man, facing the woman and taking her right hand in his, says

In the Name of God, I, *N.*, take you, *N.*, to be my wife, to have and to hold from this day forward, for better for worse, for richer for poorer, in sickness and in health, to love and to cherish, until we are parted by death. This is my solemn vow.

Then they loose their hands, and the Woman, still facing the man, takes his right hand in hers, and says

In the Name of God, I, *N.*, take you, *N.*, to be my husband, to have and to hold from this day forward, for better for worse, for richer for poorer, in sickness and in health, to love and to cherish, until we are parted by death. This is my solemn vow.

They loose their hands.

homily remembers that you are (most likely) standing to listen—and in tight, new shoes, at that. Often, the homily includes some words of encouragement, reminding us that God is willing to be a partner to this marriage, and that God can take our human efforts and bring the best from them.

The preacher can remind the various participants of the important roles they will play in your future. For the witnesses (typically the maid of honor and best man), this involves supporting you in practical ways, challenging you if you are careless about tending your marriage, standing with you when times are tough, and praying for you always. For parents and other family members, the promise to support you in your life together involves a delicate balance—being there for you when they are needed but also giving you the space you need to truly be yourselves.

THE MARRIAGE

🐾 *The Vows*

The homily will probably end with an invitation to the bride and groom to begin the exchange of their vows. Depending on the shape of your church, this may involve moving closer to the altar, or to whatever place where you will ultimately kneel for the blessing of the marriage.

Wherever the vows are performed, you will face one another directly and, taking your partner's right hand in yours (or in both your hands), make him or her your promise. I encourage couples to memorize the vows, not only because this makes the exchange seem more intimate and powerful but also because these are good words to have emblazoned on your brain for a lifetime. If even thinking about this piece of memorization makes you nervous, the officiant can read the vows to you in short pieces for you to

The Priest may ask God's blessing on a ring or rings as follows

Bless, O Lord, *this ring* to be *a sign* of the vows by which this man and this woman have bound themselves to each other; through Jesus Christ our Lord. *Amen.*

The giver places the ring on the ring-finger of the other's hand and says

N., I give you this ring as a symbol of my vow, and with all that I am, and all that I have, I honor you, in the Name of the Father, and of the Son, and of the Holy Spirit (*or* in the Name of God).

Then the Celebrant joins the right hands of husband and wife and says

Now that N. and N. have given themselves to each other by solemn vows, with the joining of hands and the giving and receiving of *a ring,* I pronounce that they are husband and wife, in the Name of the Father, and of the Son, and of the Holy Spirit.

Those whom God has joined together let no one put asunder.

People   Amen.

repeat, or you can go ahead and try memorizing them, confident that he or she will be right there with you, with an open book, in case your mind goes blank.

❧ *The Rings*

The Prayer Book wedding vows are sweeping—no good lawyer would let you sign a contract like this! We promise to have and to hold, to love and to cherish our partner no matter what the circumstances of life may bring. Such powerful vows deserve to be represented by a powerful symbol, and the traditional symbol is a ring, a circle of gold or some other metal that has no beginning or end. My parents' generation was the first to insist that not just the bride but both the man and the woman should receive a ring, that they should both wear the sign of their marriage commitment. I cannot think of any reason today, short of physical impediment, why both should not receive a ring. If you are not used to wearing a ring, it may take some getting used to. Spend some time with a friendly jeweler making sure that you have a size and shape that will be comfortable for you. Sometimes the rings are part of a matched set, but this is not at all necessary. There may be wedding rings available in your family, passed down from grandparents or great-grandparents. Such a possibility is worth asking about, especially if they had a long and happy marriage.

One of my clergy friends likes to tell people not to bother with fancy boxes for the wedding rings—you will be wearing them, not storing them! Certainly, you won't need to carry the boxes into church.

It could be said that the three foundational parts of the wedding are now complete: the hearing of Holy Scripture, the exchange of vows, and the giving and receiving of the rings. From here on, our task is to place these things in their larger setting.

The Prayers

The Deacon or other person appointed reads the following prayers, to which the People respond, saying, Amen.

Let us pray.

Eternal God, creator and preserver of all life, author of salvation, and giver of all grace: Look with favor upon the world you have made, and for which your Son gave his life, and especially upon this man and this woman whom you make one flesh in Holy Matrimony. *Amen.*

Give them wisdom and devotion in the ordering of their common life, that each may be to the other a strength in need, a counselor in perplexity, a comfort in sorrow, and a companion in joy. *Amen.*

Grant that their wills may be so knit together in your will, and their spirits in your Spirit, that they may grow in love and peace with you and one another all the days of their life. *Amen.*

Give them grace, when they hurt each other, to recognize and acknowledge their fault, and to seek each other's forgiveness and yours. *Amen.*

Make their life together a sign of Christ's love to this sinful and broken world, that unity may overcome estrangement, forgiveness heal guilt, and joy conquer despair. *Amen.*

Bestow on them, if it is your will, the gift and her- itage of children, and the grace to bring them up to know you, to love you, and to serve you. *Amen.*

Give them such fulfillment of their mutual affection that they may reach out in love and concern for others. *Amen.*

ஜ் *Tying the Knot*

When the vows have been completed, the presiding minister presents the couple to the congregation. In many congregations, it is customary for the priest to wind his or her stole around the joined hands of the couple, saying the pronouncement that they are now "husband and wife," followed by the well-known words of warning: "Those whom God has joined together let no one put asunder."

This action of winding the stole around the couple's hands seems to be the origin of the expression "tying the knot" as a colloquialism for "marrying." These words of presentation remove any need to say the words that have begun to slip into weddings from the DJ's patter at many a wedding reception: "And NOW, I present to you: Mr. and Mrs. So-and-So!" *If* the bride is taking her husband's name and *if* you really want to hear those words, in my opinion it is better to have them said at the reception.

ஜ் *The Prayers*

We then join in prayer for the couple and for the world. The prayers provided in the Prayer Book service contain much wisdom and are worth reading carefully before your wedding and often throughout your marriage, particularly on anniversaries and other special occasions. Note that the prayer for "the gift and heritage of children" is optional; couples who are clearly beyond the childbearing years will want to omit this prayer. Those who are still involved in raising children from an earlier marriage may want to use a modified version of the prayer that acknowledges the parental vocation they already have, such as one or both of the following:

> Surround them, gracious God, with the love of children [and grandchildren] and make them for us a model of love, faithfulness, and service.

Grant that all married persons who have witnessed these vows may find their lives strengthened and their loyalties confirmed. *Amen.*

Grant that the bonds of our common humanity, by which all your children are united one to another, and the living to the dead, may be so transformed by your grace, that your will may be done on earth as it is in heaven; where, O Father, with your Son and the Holy Spirit, you live and reign in perfect unity, now and for ever. *Amen.*

The Blessing of the Marriage

The people remain standing. The husband and wife kneel, and the Priest says one of the following prayers

Most gracious God, we give you thanks for your tender love in sending Jesus Christ to come among us, to be born of a human mother, and to make the way of the cross to be the way of life. We thank you, also, for consecrating the union of man and woman in his Name. By the power of your Holy Spirit, pour out the abundance of your blessing upon this man and this woman. Defend them from every enemy. Lead them into all peace. Let their love for each other be a seal upon their hearts, a mantle about their shoulders, and a crown upon their foreheads. Bless them in their work and in their companionship; in their sleeping and in their waking; in their joys and in their sorrows; in their life and in their death. Finally, in your mercy, bring them to that table where your saints feast for ever in your heavenly home; through Jesus Christ our Lord, who with you and the Holy Spirit lives and reigns, one God, for ever and ever. *Amen.*

Open their hearts to the children who will share their life and their home, and open the hearts of the children to the new thing God has done in their lives.

The prayers may be read by one of the clergy, traditionally the deacon. They may also be read by a layperson, or even better, by a number of different people. Nothing is more powerful than the prayers of those who have the greatest stake in the couple's future. Parents and grandparents, siblings and friends, whether they are members of the official wedding party or not, are all possibilities. If you choose to do the prayers this way, make a photocopy of the prayers and number each of the petitions. Then label each petition with the name of the person who will read it and make eight photocopies of your finished work. Be sure that each of your prayer leaders comes to the wedding rehearsal so they will have a chance to practice reading the prayers aloud. In most church buildings, it will be possible for them to read the prayers from wherever they are standing, especially if they are coached regarding pace and volume. If this will not work in your situation, a microphone can be provided in the aisle or at a lectern. Sometimes the bride and groom elect to read one petition themselves: the prayer asking that "all married persons who have witnessed these vows may find their lives strengthened and their loyalties confirmed." The final petition might well be read by the celebrant, following the pattern the Prayers of the People in Episcopal liturgies.

THE BLESSING OF THE MARRIAGE

The Blessing of the Marriage follows the prayers. Two forms for the blessing are provided in the 1979 Book of Common *or this*

O God, you have so consecrated the covenant
of marriage that in it is represented the spiritual
unity between Christ and his Church: Send
therefore your blessing upon these your servants,
that they may so love, honor, and cherish each
other in faithfulness and patience, in wisdom and
true godliness, that their home may be a haven of
blessing and peace; through Jesus Christ our
Lord, who lives and reigns with you and the Holy
Spirit, one God, now and for ever. *Amen.*

*The husband and wife still kneeling, the Priest adds
this blessing*

God the Father, God the Son, God the Holy
Spirit, bless, preserve, and keep you; the Lord
mercifully with his favor look upon you, and fill
you with all spiritual benediction and grace; that
you may faithfully live together in this life, and in
the age to come have life everlasting. *Amen.*

The Peace

The Celebrant may say to the people

> The peace of the Lord be always
> with you.

People　　And also with you.

*The newly married couple then greet each other, after
which greetings may be exchanged throughout the
congregation.*

Prayer. Once again, it will be helpful if you choose one, then try to articulate for your pastor why you prefer it.

The first was written in the 1970s but it incorporates some traditional imagery from the Eastern Church. It also points toward a sharing of the Eucharist in its mention of the heavenly banquet. The second is from the English Prayer Book tradition. Written in 1552, it is more abstract than the first, but contains some lovely and powerful images.

Whichever you choose, the priest concludes with a blessing in the name of God the Father, God the Son, and God the Holy Spirit.

The Peace

After the blessing, the bride and groom rise and the celebrant initiates the exchange of the Peace, beginning with the couple, whose invitation to exchange their first kiss as man and wife is "The peace of the Lord be always with you." Some scholars believe that the kiss of peace occupies the place it does in the marriage service because while the ancient custom of exchanging the peace of Christ in the eucharistic liturgy had fallen into disuse during the Middle Ages, it survived in weddings because of romantic connotations. You and your pastor will have to decide how much time to allow at this point for the exchange of the peace among your guests. It is appropriate to allow time to exchange a kiss or other greeting at least with your best man and maid of honor.

Lighting a "unity candle" is a custom that arose in situations where there was no clear and certain sacrament of unity. In a wedding where hands are taken in promise, rings are exchanged, and the Eucharist is celebrated, there is no need for such an additional ceremony.

When Communion is not to follow, the wedding party leaves the church. A hymn, psalm, or anthem may be sung, or instrumental music may be played.

THE EUCHARIST

Many weddings will now move to a celebration of the Holy Eucharist or Holy Communion. As the church's preeminent sacrament of unity, the Eucharist emphasizes the union of the newly married couple and also their connection in Christ with the others in attendance. Your first meal as man and wife will be eaten at God's altar. I like to tell couples that they are brother and sister in Christ before they are man and wife—and that there may be days when they need to fall back on this prior level of commitment.

Celebrating the Eucharist adds a bit of time to the service, but it greatly deepens the involvement of the congregation. Even with communion, your wedding will probably be much shorter than a typical Sunday church service, and it certainly seems right that it might take forty-five or fifty minutes to celebrate a lifelong commitment.

There are circumstances in which it may be appropriate to end the service here without moving to the Eucharist. These include marriages in which one member of the couple is of another faith or a nonbeliever or simply unbaptized. There are no circumstances in which it would be appropriate to give communion to the bride and groom alone, as once was done in some churches. In my experience, guests who do not receive communion because they are not of the Christian faith often report that being exposed to this part of our tradition was interesting and meaningful to them, not off-putting.

At the Eucharist

The liturgy continues with the Offertory, at which the newly married couple may present the offerings of bread and wine.

Preface of Marriage
Because in the love of wife and husband, you have given us an image of the heavenly Jerusalem, adorned as a bride for her bridegroom, your Son Jesus Christ our Lord; who loves her and gave himself for her, that he might make the whole creation new.

At the Communion, it is appropriate that the newly married couple receive Communion first, after the ministers.

🎵 The Offering of Bread and Wine

You will want to decide who brings the bread and wine of communion to the altar. These gifts come from the midst of the congregation, signifying that we are placing our lives in God's hands, just as the bread and wine are placed on the altar. The bride and groom may bring up the gifts themselves at the end of the Peace and before taking the seats that will be provided for them. Doing this acknowledges the offering of their newly joined lives to God for God's purposes. It also makes them in a sense "co-hosts" of the Eucharist with Christ, sharing in his commitment to feed and care for God's people. It is also possible to appoint members of the wedding party, family members, or church members to carry out this task. Sometimes it is the parents of the bride and groom who bring up the gifts. As the altar is being prepared, music can be played or a song can be performed by a soloist, but it is probably best for the whole congregation to sing a hymn of praise.

Some couples wish to bake the bread that will be used at their wedding, but in practice it often proves difficult to find time for this. A friend who is a proud amateur baker, however, might feel honored to be asked to provide the wedding loaf.

🎵 The Communion

Since visitors will not be familiar with the congregation's usual traffic pattern in coming forward to receive communion, it will be important to have the groomsmen, bridesmaids, or ushers prepared to offer direction. If the congregation is not too large, the bride and groom may choose to remain standing or kneeling at the rail throughout communion, so that everyone has an opportunity to be at table with them.

It is usually a good idea for the presiding minister to explain how communion will be administered. This can be done right after the peace and before the offertory sentence. Since your guests will probably include people of many dif-

In place of the usual postcommunion prayer, the following is said

O God, the giver of all that is true and lovely and gracious: We give you thanks for binding us together in these holy mysteries of the Body and Blood of your Son Jesus Christ. Grant that by your Holy Spirit, N. and N., now joined in Holy Matrimony, may become one in heart and soul, live in fidelity and peace, and obtain those eternal joys prepared for all who love you; for the sake of Jesus Christ our Lord. *Amen.*

The Bishop when present, or the Priest, may bless the people.

The Deacon, or the Celebrant, dismisses them with these words

Deacon   Go in peace to love and serve
               the Lord.

People   Thanks be to God.

As the wedding party leaves the church, a hymn, psalm, or anthem may be sung; or instrumental music may be played.

ferent denominations, he or she should also invite all baptized Christians to come forward and receive communion when the time comes (or whatever the policy in your church may be). Sometimes those who do not want to receive but who want to demonstrate their solidarity with the bride and groom are invited to come forward and kneel or stand with their arms crossed on their chest as a sign that they prefer just to receive a blessing. It is good to remember that bridesmaids and groomsmen could be in this position, too.

If there are more than a few dozen guests, it will be convenient to use the services of a second clergyperson or of some licensed eucharistic ministers. If the wedding is taking place in your home congregation, you may be able to suggest to your pastor which of the available eucharistic ministers you would like to see invited.

GOING FORTH

⮞ *The Postcommunion Prayer*
When all have received communion, the wedding party gathers once again in the position where the service began. From this spot (however they get there), the celebrant will lead the whole congregation in saying the special postcommunion prayer provided in the marriage service.

⮞ *The Dismissal*
The bride and groom are then sent forth into the world as a new couple and, along with the congregation, as representatives of Christ. The best Prayer Book dismissal for this purpose is probably: "Go in peace to love and serve the Lord." The congregation responds with a hearty "Thanks be to God"—something that needs to be practiced at the rehearsal lest the final words heard at the wedding be weak and fal-

tering because everyone's attention is on the procession that is about to take place.

Be sure that you know where you are going to go when you reach the church door. You will probably not want to stop in the entryway and form a receiving line unless you have a significant number of guests who will not be coming to the reception. Find an out-of-the-way place to wait until the guests have exited, especially if you will be returning to the church to take photos. Do not make the mistake of having ushers return to lead parents and other honored members of the wedding party out of the church. Although this may add to the sense of solemnity and anticipation when it is done before the service, it will prove maddeningly stiff and anticlimactic afterward. Ask the family members to simply fall in behind the members of the wedding party as you all make your exit.

One thing that ought to be mentioned here, perhaps, is the custom of certain military and fraternal groups to provide a "sword arch" or some other festive gateway for the newly married couple to pass through as they exit the church. This custom is often spoiled by the insistence of the last of the sword-bearers on giving the bride a whack on the rump with the broadside of his sword. If you find this demeaning (as most women do) but still wish to have the archway, be sure to negotiate with sword-bearers ahead of time about eliminating it.

6

Other Things to Think About

PREMARITAL COUNSELING

It is a norm in most denominations for you and your pastor to work together through a process of premarital counseling. The purpose of this counseling is not for the pastor to make a judgment about the validity of your decision to marry (although it does occasionally happen that a clergyperson will decline to marry a couple, or a couple will recognize in the course of the counseling that they have more work to do before marriage is appropriate). Rather, the counseling is intended to raise your awareness of the strengths of your relationship and to help you take account of the particular challenges you may face. Although each clergyperson has his or her own way of doing this work, your counseling is likely to include the following:

- a look at the families you come from and their particular dynamics;
- an examination of the way you see yourself and your partner, possibly using a testing instrument such as the Taylor-Johnson Temperament Analysis;
- discussion of some of the topics especially relevant to a new marriage, such as the use of money, sexual expression, gender roles, priorities, and values;
- some teaching about the church's understanding of marriage and God's calling to you as married persons.

If it is available in your area, it would also be a good idea to take the Myers-Briggs Type Indicator and discuss it with someone familiar with the marital application of personality type. If you cannot find anyone to do it with you, the books *Please Understand Me: Character and Temperament Types* by Marilyn Bates and David Keirsey or *Please Understand Me II* by David Keirsey might be of help in doing the work yourselves.

Finally, of course, premarital counseling is intended to help you begin or deepen a pastoral relationship with the person who will preside at your wedding and to provide a context for your planning the wedding together with your pastor.

In those cases where the actual ceremony will take place away from your home faith community, there may need to be a division of pastoral labor. Ask the person with whom you will have the ongoing pastoral connection to do your premarital counseling, even if someone else will be presiding at the wedding. If you are going elsewhere for the wedding— back to your hometown, for example—do not make assumptions about what the pastor there knows or how he or she does things. Talk with your pastor about your vision of the wedding, then plan the details with the person who will be presiding. If you can afford to cover the cost of his or her travel and lodging, consider asking your pastor to come along and participate, with the blessing, of course, of the person who will preside.

THE REHEARSAL

A rehearsal will be essential for all but the simplest of weddings. Walking through the service ahead of time will make it possible for you and your supporters to give your full attention to the wedding when it actually takes place, rather than worrying about unresolved details. The goal of a good rehearsal is for you to become clear enough about what will be happening that you can be fully present at your own wedding: to hear the music, to see the people gathered, to hear the lessons and homily, then to give yourself with heart and soul to your spouse and to God in the vows and in the Eucharist. It is difficult to do this if you are distracted by uncertainties.

❧ *Who Runs the Rehearsal?*
Today's wedding industry has spawned the role of wedding consultant or wedding director, a person whose job is presumably to walk you through the myriad details and costly decisions the wedding professionals hope you will make. Perhaps you have already discovered that there are also a bountiful number of amateurs willing to give you their advice and experience. Engage one of these people to help with the reception, if you must, but please be clear that they have no place at the wedding or wedding rehearsal. The member of the clergy presiding at your wedding will be in charge of your rehearsal, assisted perhaps by one or more members of the congregation.

❧ *Who Should Attend?*

In addition to the bride and groom, parents need to be present so they are comfortable and well-informed about what will actually happen at your wedding. Insist on this. Bridesmaids and groomsmen, other attendants, and ushers all need to be there as well. Grandparents and others who will be seated in some ceremonial fashion should be present if possible. Those reading Scripture lessons should be present and prepared to actually read through their lesson at the rehearsal, as should all who may have been asked to help with the prayers. If the chalice bearers for the Eucharist are not members of the local congregation, they should be present as well. Your clergy person will decide whether or not the crucifer and acolytes need to come to the rehearsal.

❧ *Setting the Time*

Your pastor can tell you approximately how long your rehearsal will take. If you will be having a rehearsal dinner afterward, be sure to allow adequate transportation time for you and your wedding party to get safely to your destination. How long the rehearsal takes depends partly on when it starts. If you have people in your wedding party who are habitually late, give them an earlier target time all their own. Do whatever it takes to get people assembled on time. If members of the wedding party are coming to the rehearsal from the golf course or some other social setting, make it clear that they must not do any drinking. Loud, disruptive, or unsteady wedding participants cannot learn their parts well and they could make the rehearsal long and unpleasant for others.

❧ *The Rehearsal Dinner*

As a person who attends lots of rehearsal dinners and wedding receptions, I hear a lot of dumb and embarrassing toasts. Some are downright offensive. And for the most part, these violations of good taste and human kindness happen because of a lack of preparation. People need instruction about toasts and someone needs to be in charge of making them. Send a note ahead of time to those who may be asked to say something. List the areas that are—and are not— appropriate for comment. (Hard as it is to believe, comparisons with former boyfriends or girlfriends, comments about breast or penis size, and advice-giving in general need to be specifically proscribed.) Let speakers know that it does not hurt to actually make some notes or write a toast out on paper. They can always add spontaneous comments later. Appoint someone you trust to be master of ceremonies and actually talk with him or her about what you hope will— and will not—happen.

I once went to a wedding in Pittsburgh at which the bride's Canadian relatives all showed up with typewritten toasts on index cards. I thought to myself, "What an uptight bunch!" Well, those toasts turned out to be the most meaningful and loving tributes I have ever heard. It may be that the best chance of celebrating your union with truly memorable toasts is at the rehearsal dinner. Give your friends and family some coaching, and these could be some of the best moments in the whole wedding celebration.

It should be noted that families can have very different expectations about the place of alcoholic drinks in celebrations of all sorts. Some families may believe you cannot celebrate without drinking; for others, booze will be completely out of bounds. To complicate things further, almost every family has certain members who should not drink or cannot drink appropriately. In this matter, the bride and groom must lead the way in displaying sensitivity. If there is a clear division of responsibility for the different wedding events, then it may be appropriate that the customs of those in charge be followed. In any situation where alcohol will be served, it is important that attractive alternatives be provided. This is especially important at times when toasts will be offered or, for some other reason, everyone is expected to have a glass in his or her hand. If there will be cases of champagne, make sure there are cases of sparkling cider on hand as well. My own experience in party planning is that when there are appealing alternatives, you will always be impressed at how many people choose them.

PHOTOGRAPHY

My family greatly values the wedding-day photographs we have of some of our ancestors. It would appear that these good people posed for a single picture, perhaps in a photographer's studio. Today, however, photographers often attempt to document every aspect of a wedding or a wedding weekend, from dawn to dusk. Let me offer a few thoughts about how to handle this.

If you think you want to use a professional wedding photographer, seek recommendations from people who have been married recently. If you must pick a photographer out of the phone book, ask for the names of recent clients. The questions you want to ask are: (1) Were you pleased with the quality and timely delivery of the finished photos; and (2) Was the photographer unobtrusive and cooperative during the festivities? Competent professionals will make time to meet with you, not only to sell their services but also to find out what you do and do not want them to do. In the photographers' defense, their worst nightmare is hearing the bride or groom ask after the wedding, "Why didn't you get a photo of . . . whatever?" They therefore tend to err on the side of taking photos of everything! Also, in the absence of a better plan, your photographer will happily run the wedding, taking you from one opportunity to pose to the next, but unfortunately isolating you from your guests and the real celebration of the day.

Take the time to plan specific photos with your professional. In most churches, there are severe limits placed on photography during the service. These rules are intended to make sure that everyone, from the wedding guests to the bride and groom, can pay attention to what is actually taking place rather than the efforts to record it.

Some parishes permit weddings to be videotaped or allow non-flash photos from the rear of the church. Even in such cases, you will still probably need to take fifteen or twenty minutes following the service to pose for pictures. Remember that your guests and members of the church's altar guild are waiting for you to finish. It is often better to take your photos *before* the service, so your exit from the church can be the real thing. A videotape or audiotape of your wedding is a nice thing to have; if you wish to have such a remembrance be sure to arrange for it ahead of time. We have a local film production company that prepares a beautiful, professionally edited tape, but their many large cameras can be a bit obtrusive. In some places, a tape can be made using the same cameras and microphones that record services on Sundays.

Some photographers will come to your rehearsal. While this is not necessary, it may help them to envision the photos they want to pose in the brief time allotted for them.

SUPERSTITIONS AND TRADITIONS

Traditions are a great thing. Good traditions can help us remember who we are and where we have come from because they incorporate glimpses of the truth about us. Superstitions, on the other hand, have no basis in our best vision of ourselves and our lives. Instead, they play on our fears and uncertainties.

One prevalent superstition is the idea that it is unlucky for the bride and groom to see each other before they meet at the altar. This is a reflection, of course, of the days when some unfortunate wedding partners really could find themselves at the chancel step facing a future spouse chosen by others, someone they had hardly even seen before. It denies the very earnest discernment that a bride and groom have gone through *together* before this day was ever imagined. While it may be very wise for the bride and groom to have totally separate places to prepare for the wedding, there are several times in the day when the couple may choose to be together.

The bride and groom might, for example, elect to have a private breakfast or brunch together. An unintended consequence of our current wedding customs is that the bride and groom may have their time so closely scheduled in the days right before the wedding that they hardly see each other. I remember barely getting to speak to my wife-to-be at the rehearsal dinner and party. In the emotionally charged atmosphere caused by the collision of large numbers of friends and relatives from two families who are still getting to know each other, the bride and groom are likely to have plenty to talk about! Why not build in a quiet hour or two before the rush of preparation begins in earnest?

The other time the bride and groom might come together is before the wedding procession. In some cases, the bride and groom may elect to welcome their guests themselves at the entrance to the church. This is an especially good idea when many of the wedding guests will arrive at the church without having seen the bride and groom for some time. The bride and groom might want to include parents in the greeting process. Be sure to build into your planning the time this will take and be prepared to extricate yourselves from the greeting ten minutes or so before the wedding begins, so that you have time for final preparations and a prayer together.

Another superstition, possibly related to the idea that one intends to say the wedding vows only once in a lifetime, dissuaded couples from practicing the vows at the wedding rehearsal. Sometimes there was even a stand-in for the bride! Today, we are of the opinion that saying those vows repeatedly is a good idea; we want them to sink as deeply into our hearts and minds as possible.

Your pastor can help you sort through the other traditions that may be held up to you as important, so that you can decide whether honoring them supports or actually undermines the integrity of your wedding. Just ask.

MONEY MATTERS

✍ *Fees*

Most churches will ask that you cover the actual costs of your wedding by paying the maintenance person who opens up and cleans up, the musician or musicians who play or sing for your service, the costs incurred by the altar guild, and so on. There is usually a printed schedule of such expenses. In addition, there may be a fee that represents a gift to the church over and above the actual costs that you are covering. This fee could vary depending on whether you are actual church members who already contribute to its work, or guests who do not. If no such fee is expected, as would be the case in my own church, you might like to consider making the church a monetary gift in thanksgiving for the gift God has given you in one another. Ten percent of the total cost of the wedding (a tithe) would be a guide.

Sometimes a fee for the pastor will be included in the schedule of fees, but it will often not be. Remember that the minister leading your service has likely spent hours planning and counseling with you and will spend hours more at your rehearsal and wedding. If you are not sure about an appropriate amount, you might take the organist's fee and double it. It is great to invite the minister and his or her spouse to the reception and/or to the rehearsal dinner, if you really want him or her to be there. Please do not think of this as a perk, however. Your pastor may be delighted to come, but for most clergy such events really do represent two more nights "on duty."

How Much is Enough?

The cost of your wedding is worth discussing. People who get married in a no-cost wedding are just as married as those who spend thousands. There are many ways to control the cost of a wedding. One is to consider less than formal clothing: suits and dresses you can actually wear again, as opposed to items that must be rented or worn only once. Another is to shop local thrift shops for your wedding gown.

If it will not complicate the travel of too many people, another cost-saving measure is to consider having your wedding at some time other than Saturday night. Party centers are often empty on Friday nights or Sunday nights; restaurants are often closed on Mondays and less busy on weeknights than weekends. Whatever the time of your wedding, holding your reception in the church parish hall will cost far less than a party center or restaurant. You may have friends who would love to provide beverages or foods they can cook in lieu of some other kind of wedding gift. Be sure to find out ahead of time what the church's rules are regarding costs, alcoholic beverages, reception times, kitchen use, and clean-up.

If you do not expect to invite a huge number of guests, your host congregation might even enjoy the opportunity to celebrate your marriage on a Sunday morning at one of the regular service times. For the church, it would be an educational opportunity. For you, it would be a way to celebrate with a big crowd at little cost. You could help make the after-service coffee hour one of the best ever!

Whatever level of expense you decide is appropriate, consider *tithing* on the total cost; that is, giving ten percent of what will be spent on the wedding to the church or a charity. If this amount seems recklessly generous to you, think again about the cost of the whole wedding.

Who Will Pay?

The question of *who will pay* for the wedding should also be discussed. Families can have vastly different resources, so while the tradition remains that the wedding and reception are the responsibility of the bride's family and the rehearsal dinner (if any) the province of the groom's, the reality is that financial responsibilities can be shared by the couple and their respective families in any way you work out. It is not uncommon for the bride's parents to be divorced and remarried to spouses with children and expectations of their own. So some couples will be dealing with three or four sets of "parents" rather than just one or two. Grandparents are also often involved. Although they certainly bring their own, more ancient, expectations about weddings, my experience is that they are often better than parents at letting go and allowing couples to craft the wedding they want.

In a perfect world, parents who are going to help pay for a wedding would say, "Here is what we can provide; just let us know when you want the check." In reality, however, a certain amount of control often goes with the gift of financial aid. At their worst, weddings can become parties parents put on for their friends. In their defense, some parents *do* have friends who will bring their own expectations: "All our children get married under the gazebo at the country club," or "How are we going to do any line dancing if you don't have the reception at the party center?" Try to check out everyone's expectations as best you can. Many couples have discovered that, when all is said and done, they would have preferred a simple, low-cost wedding to the elaborate wedding they had, with many strings attached. My suggestion is this: if you have to compromise your principles, do so in regard to the reception and make the service more completely your own.

🎵 *Wedding Gifts*

Stores have thought of everything to help couples let it be known what they need and do not need in the way of gifts. One thing they cannot accept is the reality that many couples come to marriage with all the kitchen gear they need and no interest in silver or china. More and more wedding invitations specify "No gifts, please!" If this applies to you, take note. There are two other possibilities. One is to specify a charity. The other is to invite gifts to a wedding or honeymoon fund. This is especially appropriate when the bride and groom are students or otherwise obviously unable to fund such an adventure.

LEGAL MATTERS

🎵 *Prenuptial Agreements*

Many people are generally uncomfortable with the idea of prenuptial agreements, and with good reason. They often represent reservations that need to be carefully examined. If you are considering a prenuptial agreement, be sure to discuss this with your pastor to make sure it is compatible with the vows you are about to make.

There are instances, however, in which such agreements can be a good idea. When there are children from previous marriages whose rights need to be clarified and whose needs should be respected, a prenuptial agreement may be important. If either of you is the owner or part-owner of significant family property or a family business, a prenuptial agreement may be in order to protect the interests of other members of the family. Finally, if you have responsibilities such as the care of an elderly parent or a disabled sibling, a prenuptial agreement can clarify how much of this responsibility your new spouse is expected to share. If any of this sounds like your situation, see a lawyer.

⅋ *Your Will*

While most people do not need a prenuptial agreement, *everyone* needs a will. If you already have one, it will need to be updated to reflect your new marital status. There will be questions to answer about who acquires your assets or deals with your debts in the event of your death. The answers to these questions may in some cases involve the purchase of some additional life insurance. If you have never had a will before, prepare one now. It's best to see a lawyer, but even the will from a computer program is better than nothing.

Deal with your will *before* the wedding, making it effective on your wedding day. It would be foolish to ignore the many instances of people dying in the first months of marriage or even on their honeymoon. Get it done. It could save untold pain and suffering for your spouse later, who in the midst of grieving for you might be in a seriously compromised financial situation. Perhaps clergy should insist on seeing a new will before they start the ceremony!

⅋ *Marriage Documents*

On one of your visits to the church, you will be asked to sign a "Declaration of Intention":

> We, N. N. and N. N., desiring to receive the blessing of Holy Matrimony in the Church, do solemnly declare that we hold marriage to be a lifelong union of husband and wife as it is set forth in the Book of Common Prayer.

We believe that the union of husband and wife,
in heart, body, and mind, is intended by God for
their mutual joy; for the help and comfort given one
another in prosperity and adversity; and, when it is
God's will, for the procreation of children and their
nurture in the knowledge and love of the Lord.

And we do engage ourselves, so far as in us lies,
to make our utmost effort to establish this relationship and to seek God's help thereto.

Although historically the Declaration was probably related
to the publishing of the banns, today it represents a covenant
of understanding between the couple and the church regarding the nature of marriage. It says unequivocally that those
seeking to be married hold marriage "to be a lifelong union"
and that they are prepared to make such a commitment.
There really are people who marry thinking, "Let's give it a
try and see what happens." That sort of marriage may be
their choice, but it is not what the church means by marriage.

Some time right before or after the service, you will probably be invited to sign a page in the parish's register of services that contains the essential information about you and
your marriage. Although this is a holdover from the days
when the church was the only reliable record keeper for matters such as marriage, the Marriage Register still provides a
useful backup record of the promises and vows you will
make. Your principal witnesses will sign, too.

Marriage license procedures vary from state to state. Be
sure to find out what you need to do and what you will need
to bring to the licensing agency's office in the jurisdiction
where you will be married. Sometimes waiting periods exist.
Often you need to present a birth certificate. In some states
you get a discount if you can prove that you have done some
serious premarital counseling, so you may need a letter from
your pastor. Licenses are typically good for thirty or sixty

days, so this may be something you can take care of ahead of time. But don't forget. Without a license, the minister really cannot marry you!

HONEYMOONS

The big question to ask about a honeymoon is: Is it *you*? The purpose of a post-wedding trip is to give the bride and groom some unpressured time together after the busyness of the wedding. Your honeymoon may also be an opportunity to do something together that you have long envisioned as a couple, like a visit to Tahiti or a rafting trip on the Colorado River. Just be sure that, as with your wedding, what you plan is true to who you are. If you are not people who would usually consider going to an "all-inclusive" Caribbean resort, you may not want to do that for your honeymoon.

Cost matters too. It may take all the fun out of a trip if you know that you are going to be paying for it for years. Do something within your means, and you are much more likely to enjoy it now and look back on it fondly. Even if you have no financial constraints, make sure you will be comfortable with what you choose. Sometimes there can be a fine line between celebratory luxury and embarrassing excess.

Since, in this day and age, the honeymoon is not likely to be needed as a "get-acquainted" time, it certainly can be postponed until a time when it fits into your lives and schedules. You will, however, lose the chance to use the honeymoon as a "wedding recovery" time.

Consider alternatives too. The best honeymoon for you may not involve going away. I have fond memories of a wedding held years ago in Maine at which the bride and groom, who would be living overseas for the foreseeable future, decided they wanted to spend their post-wedding days with their friends and family. Friends and neighbors lent their homes and skills for three days of kite-flying, lobster bakes, and ongoing celebration, as the bride and groom enjoyed the Maine coast and their loved ones.

DEALING WITH FAMILY EXPECTATIONS

When a wedding is approaching, family members will behave as they normally do—only more so! Dominating mothers will dominate away, nosy siblings will butt in, and absent fathers will absent themselves. Pay attention and learn! Whether your impending marriage feels to family members like a blessing or a nightmare, it definitely qualifies in family systems theory as a "life-crisis event." As such, it is one of those times when the unwritten rules of life in your family will be closest to the surface. It is also a time—believe it or not—when those rules are most subject to change.

Let me begin by stating the obvious: it is *your* wedding. There are certainly couples who can only wish their parents were alive to participate—or interested enough to meddle. But it is more likely that family members will have expectations you have to deal with. If you are inclined to hope that if you just "go along" with the plans, the wedding and its related celebrations will be the "one last time" you get treated like an extension of your family rather than an independent adult, think again. It is far more likely that the tone of your wedding preparations will set the direction of your relationship with your birth families for some time to come. So bite the bullet. Step up to the plate. Face the music. Take charge.

Start by collecting some information. If there have been recent family weddings, say of older siblings or cousins, then there may be some clear precedents. Parents may have expectations that they have nourished for many years. Be cagey with your family. Conduct a series of interviews. Sit down with parents and others who may feel that they should be consulted, and consult them. Listen hard, take notes, smile frequently, but say little. Insist that you are still in the discernment mode yourselves because there is a lot to think about and the wedding really does make a statement about who you are and want to be. Be sure to close by asking if there is anything else your advisors want to tell you. Then, thank them profusely and promise to report back soon.

What are the family traditions on both sides? Knowing these things can be helpful. In most cases, you will find it really *is not* true that "we have always done things this way," because in reality, weddings were often much simpler a generation or two ago. In most families, you do not have to look far to find the example of a couple who got married on their lunch hour because money was scarce during the Great Depression, or a bride who did not wear the ancestral gown because she was too pregnant. There may be family traditions that will mean a great deal to you, like serving beans and rice and homemade tacos at the reception, or having all the men in the wedding party wear kilts. The important thing is that you are able to pick and choose among them.

If your wedding vision is profoundly and irreconcilably different from your family's, getting married privately in a distant place should not be ruled out. If you decide to do this, you can still take advantage of the premarital counseling offered by your church, and your pastor may be able to help you arrange a wedding in Jamaica, Canada, or Mexico with a local clergyperson presiding. If at all possible, you should look on the wedding as a time for everyone to take account of the fact that your primary allegiance is no longer to your family of origin but to your new spouse. For good or ill, patterns set at the wedding will long endure.

7

Unusual and Nontraditional Weddings

*D*o you think of your coming marriage as somehow unusual? Are you perhaps even wondering whether a church wedding is appropriate? If so, this chapter is for you.

As a matter of fact, of all the new marriages that took place in the United States in a recent year, fewer than 50 percent were between a childless man and woman under age thirty who had never been married before. The people who celebrate their marriages in churches today represent a full and fascinating cross-section of our national life. It may be that all they have in common is their passionate commitment to one another and their conviction that marriage vows need to be anchored in their faith. Even if you do not find your situation described below, it will still be worthwhile for you to talk with a clergyperson about your hopes and plans. You may be pleasantly surprised at the various forms of support the church has to offer.

DIVORCED PERSONS

Since 1973, the Episcopal Church, like many other churches, has had a process by which people who have been married and divorced can apply for permission to be married in the church. This is the church's way of affirming that people can learn and grow from their losses while at the same time insisting that marriage really *is* meant to be a lifelong commitment. The process of seeking this permission from your diocesan bishop is not as onerous as it might sound. It is mostly handled face-to-face with the pastor who is doing your premarital counseling.

In fact, unlike an annulment process, which might be construed as an effort to set aside your previous marriage and declare that in the church's eyes it was defective or never existed, the Episcopal Church's remarriage process takes your previous marriage seriously. It asks that you look honestly at the reasons it failed—to the extent that this is under your control—and takes into consideration how you have dealt with these issues. If, for example, you were an active alcoholic during the breakup of your first marriage, your pastor will want you to describe your progress in recovery. Painful as it may be, discussing your previous marriage openly with your pastor and your wife- or husband-to-be is very useful. My experience is that although most couples have tried to be open with one another about their marital history, much remains to be learned. Because the end of a marriage is usually so painful, it is not something we relish thinking about, and the chance to reflect from within the safety and distance of a new love relationship can produce wisdom, clarity, and possibly even forgiveness.

The church's canons (written laws or official procedures) expect that at least one year will have elapsed between your final decree of divorce and the proposed date of your new marriage. If this is not true for you, make sure your priest knows this right away. You might be counseled to wait until more time has elapsed, or to go ahead and contract a civil marriage while scheduling a service of blessing for a future date. The option of having a civil marriage now and a service of blessing later might be appropriate, for example, in the case of a person in the military who has a long deployment pending and whose new spouse needs to be brought under his or her insurance coverage right away.

A wedding in which one or both persons have been previously married may not look any different from a marriage ceremony between two never-married persons. It is perfectly all right in this day and age for the bride to wear white and for the gentlemen to wear formal attire—if that is what you really want to do. In my experience, men and women who have been married before are often better able to focus on the interpersonal and spiritual aspects of a wedding than they were at an earlier time in their lives. More energy goes into planning who needs to be present, what Scripture passages will be read, and how the gift of this relationship will be celebrated. I suggest that, even if you are keeping things very simple, a best man and maid of honor (better called "witnesses") still be designated to serve as the official witnesses to your vows, but it may make sense to have other attendants, too. In a sense, the whole congregation you assemble will serve as your attendants and witnesses. As the Prayer Book service reminds us at the very beginning of the service, "We have come together in the presence of God to witness and bless the joining together of this man and this woman in Holy Matrimony."

If it is the case that only one of you has been previously married, the partner who has never been married may have some long-cherished visions of their wedding that will now have to be evaluated. How can you honor some of these expectations, while also acknowledging your spouse-to-be's possible desire *not* to walk down the aisle in a white dress or pose on the chancel steps with a row of groomsmen in cutaways? As with every wedding, it will be important to sort out what you as a couple need and want versus what family members may expect. Then it will be possible to negotiate with them in a thoughtful way.

THE ROLE OF CHILDREN

If you have children from your previous marriage, including them in your marriage celebration can be a wonderful way to acknowledge the history that you bring to this special day. For young children, the most important thing is that they be present. Certainly, they can be ring bearers and flower girls, but such an official role is not necessary. Sometimes young children can stand with the other official witnesses during the exchange of the vows, but it is probably not reasonable to expect them to stand before the congregation for the whole service. They will need someone to sit with, someone with whom they are very comfortable.

Older children can participate in many more ways. They can read a Scripture lesson, serve as an acolyte, or simply sit in the congregation. It is important to respect the overwhelming mixture of feelings that your children may feel on this day, no matter how much you would like them simply to be happy and no matter how much they may like your new spouse. They may be very excited and hopeful about the marriage, and at the same time fearful of the unknown changes that lie ahead. They may bring sadness from the loss of their previous family structure, a desire to protect their parent from future disappointments—a myriad of thoughts and emotions. Take your cue from them and consult them as much as possible about your plans, without giving them veto power over anything except their own participation. You have a right to insist that your children be there on your big day—but that is all. Adult children can be a great source of support, but they will bring the same mixed bag of emotions as younger kids.

I have known a number of couples who have asked a former spouse to be in attendance at the wedding. Go gently with this, even if he or she has become a good and trusted friend. This is a tough role to play. A friend of mine recently invited her former husband to come and take part in the wedding and reception—but she declined his offer to walk her to the altar, as this was a little more than she could bear. He was grateful to be included and worked hard to make himself useful during the party that followed.

Whether your children take part in the wedding or not, during the prayers of the people it is a good idea to include one of the alternative prayers that mentions the role of children in the new couple's life, as suggested in chapter 5.

WIDOWS AND WIDOWERS

Many of the issues discussed above apply to weddings where one or both parties had a marriage that was ended by the death of their spouse. Although the canons do not specifically require it, it is important for widows and widowers to talk in some depth with their pastor about their previous experience of marriage and the ways in which they think the new marriage will and will not be like the earlier one. Although you are certainly aware that this is a new relationship, there may be subtle ways in which you expect or yearn for married life to go forward in the old, familiar way.

One way to help both you and your new spouse take account of the change in your life is to find a new home together. Although this will not necessarily be an economically sound idea, the process of finding and preparing a new place to live can help build a new foundation. If you decide that you will live in a home that already belongs to one of you, talk with your pastor about how you are going to make it belong to you as a couple. Part of your engagement process or the wedding festivities could be a service for the blessing of your new home.

The process of planning your wedding can help bring to the surface your assumptions about the life you will share. It may be tempting to skip over some of the usual wedding customs, but talking together about the same questions that first-time marriage candidates work through will be useful. How many people should you include in your celebration? Who, if anyone, needs to stand with you as you make your vows? How will you celebrate? All these details are important both in themselves and for the conversations they can begin.

OLDER COUPLES

Older persons who fall in love and want to share a life together may face a number of special concerns. Sometimes pensions or other forms of income are dependent on the individual's remaining single. Perceiving this to be an injustice, some clergy have been willing to perform a blessing without benefit of marriage license. Although their motive is understandable, this is a very questionable practice for a number of reasons. In some states, the ceremony could lead to the acknowledgment of a common-law marriage with all the negative financial consequences the couple sought to avoid.

Such a practice is also confusing to family members and to the couple themselves. What happens when one of the two dies? Is there an expectation that the survivor will have some claim on the resources and the family of their deceased partner? If so, it would be better to resolve such questions through a will and a trust, or perhaps through simply getting married. Every bride and groom should prepare new wills; this is especially important for older couples. And however you resolve the legal and financial issues you have, your family members will be better served by clarity than confusion. Tell them exactly what you are doing, and they can probably come to terms with it.

In my experience, family members and friends are often more supportive of the new alliance than the partners expect they will be. The Prayer Book marriage liturgy itself is perfectly appropriate for the marriage of older persons, though some of our traditions are not. I suggest that if there is a need for the wedding to begin with a procession, the bride and groom enter together. Seating should be provided for the bride and groom, as well as for their witnesses. Be sure to omit the petition for the gift and heritage of children from the prayers of the people, or amend it as suggested earlier in chapter 5.

COUPLES OF WIDELY DIFFERENT AGES

One of my all-time favorite weddings involved a forty-year-old bride who was twice-divorced and a sixty-year-old groom whose first wife I had known and cared for until her death a few years earlier. This bride and groom were eager to plan the wedding and get on with their lives, but they tried to be patient with all the things the church asked of them. The conversations we had about previous marriages that had failed were sad and somewhat painful, but they enabled me to tell our bishop that I believed the bride was really able—at last—to fulfill the promise of a lifelong union. The groom was a very private person but he tried heroically to express his sense of loss and hope as we talked about the blessings and challenges that might lie ahead.

Although this couple were inclined to keep their wedding simple and small, the more they thought about the ceremony, the more they realized many lives would be touched and changed by the promises they were about to make. The bride had a teenaged son who needed to be included in some way, and many business colleagues who were also genuine friends. The groom had a number of grown children who brought many different feelings to the day, including excitement and hope, a sense of protectiveness for their father, and a sense of loss from their mother's death that was still raw some days. The counseling sessions, the wedding, the reception, and the associated family gatherings turned out to be a bigger undertaking than the two had ever imagined, but they proved to be a good foundation for a marriage that has lasted more than twenty years now.

Wedding customs really do change greatly as time passes. What was typical when many of one's peers were getting married twenty, thirty, or forty years ago may have changed greatly. Thank goodness, no matter what the difference in age, a couple who share a religious tradition will have a language in common for celebrating what is most important to them. Make the most of the religious aspects of your celebration!

SAME-SEX COUPLES

The church strives to put marriage in the context of a community where decisions can be tested, support can be given, and celebrations shared. As I write this book, it is not clear whether or not the Episcopal Church will choose to officially authorize the blessing of same-sex unions. However, more and more clergy and congregations are finding ways to provide community support for people in same-sex relationships who understand their commitment in the context of their Christian faith. How much the church has to offer you will depend partly on where you live. Certain Episcopal dioceses have gone ahead with blessing services, with particular parishes leading the way; others will not perform such blessings but might be open to other celebrations or expressions of support. To find out what is possible, start with your own pastor, if you have one. If not, ask around. The mainline church that is most open to hosting same-sex blessing services is the United Church of Christ, the Congregational church. Other denominations are in various states of struggle over what to do.

In my opinion, a public blessing ceremony held in the church needs to have the support of a comfortable majority of the congregation's members if it is to be meaningful. I understand whatever authority I have to pardon or to bless as flowing from the community that ordained and called me. If you are the first to seek such a public service of blessing in a particular congregation, expect to take part in a (possibly lengthy) process of seeking support, first from the congregation's vestry and then perhaps from the congregation as a whole. Finally, it will be up to your pastor to let the bishop of the diocese know what is being planned. In some dioceses, the bishop will be openly supportive. In other places it would be best not to ask the bishop's permission but simply to keep the bishop informed, thus providing him or her the option (which we hope would not be exercised) of specifically admonishing your pastor not to go ahead. In yet other dioceses, the clergy will know that performing a public blessing ceremony is out of the question. Talk with your pastor about what is possible in your area for same-sex partners who are ready to make a lifelong commitment.

If you are looking for a private prayer service of some sort held in your home, many clergy would be able and willing to do this, perhaps following the pattern found in the rite for the Celebration for a Home in *The Book of Occasional Services*. In this service, the couple whose home is being blessed moves from room to room with their pastor and as many friends and family members as they choose to include. This can be great fun! In each room, prayers are offered for the daily activities that happen there, from washing in the bathrooms to cooking in the kitchen. When all the rooms have been blessed by prayer, the presence of friends, and possibly a sprinkling of holy water, the whole company gathers in the main living area for the blessing of the home. This is the time when the two people who will live in this home can voice their intention to share their lives. When they have done this, the presiding minister blesses the home that they will share. The service concludes, if desired, with the celebration of the Holy Eucharist. A meal or reception may follow.

Liturgical models for same-sex blessings are available from several dioceses. Some services parallel closely the Prayer Book service for the Celebration and Blessing of a Marriage. Others are quite different, but they are still likely to contain the reading of Holy Scripture, the couple's exchange of vows, and the invocation of the Holy Spirit in a prayer of blessing. Holy Communion, our great sacrament of unity, may be celebrated as well.

The language of the Declaration of Intention used in the Episcopal Church is not appropriate for use by same-sex couples. In the case of a same-sex blessing, it is perhaps even more important that we be clear about what we intend. Until dioceses establish policies, parishes that perform such blessings might consider asking couples to sign the following amended Declaration:

> We, *N. N.* and *N. N.*, desiring to receive the blessing of our relationship in the church, do solemnly declare that we intend a lifelong union under the Lordship of Christ.
> We believe that the union of two human beings, in heart, body, and mind, is intended by God for their mutual joy; for the help and comfort given one another in prosperity and adversity; and for the opportunity to contribute together to the growth of God's kingdom.
> And we do engage ourselves, so far as in us lies, to make our utmost effort to establish this relationship and to seek God's help thereto.

Instead of worrying about less important customs exported from wedding tradition, such as who will be in the procession and what people will wear, try to focus on the essentials. Here's what I suggest: Let everyone be seated. Put the couple on opposite sides of the aisle or provide seats for them—together—somewhere in the chancel. Let the whole congregation enjoy the music that is being played and pray silently for the two people they have come to support. When the music ends, let the person who is presiding stand to welcome people and remind them why they have gathered. Then Holy Scripture is read, a homily is preached, vows are exchanged, prayers are prayed, and a blessing is given. Holy Communion is shared. When the service is simple and powerful, even those who were not sure how they might feel about participating will come away saying, "This was a great experience; I am glad I was there." And the new couple will know they have the support of their faith community.

Whatever the liturgical options available in your area, I suggest that the same sort of counseling process should be undertaken as is provided to male-female couples, so that potential partners can assess the strengths and challenges their union will face and gather the resources to respond to them. Just as with heterosexual couples, same-sex partners who have already lived together for some time report that making vows before God and their friends changes things. How will you be changed by a formal public ritual that places your commitment to your partner in the context of your commitment to Christ?

I have asked some same-sex couples in my own congregation why they have never talked with me about celebrating their union in the church that means so much to them. They almost universally have told me: "We did not want to put you in a difficult position." It really is okay to talk with your pastor about your hopes and plans. Most likely, he or she will feel honored to know about your vision for your life together, and you may find that the church is better able to respond than you expected.

COUPLES FROM DIFFERENT RELIGIOUS TRADITIONS

Every couple will bring different faith assumptions to their wedding, even if they come from the same religion and denomination. When their traditions are quite different, however, the issues become more complex, both for the day of the wedding and for how the new couple will practice their faith in the years to come. It may be helpful to seek out other couples who have brought together faith traditions similar to yours and see what you can learn from their experience.

It was once common for Protestant and Catholic Christians to continue to practice their separate faith traditions after their marriage. In every congregation I have served, there have been one or more couples, usually married prior to 1970, who have done this. I especially remember one couple who for twenty years had gone to the early Eucharist at their separate churches each week and met afterward for breakfast. Once their churches began using the same lectionary, they enjoyed comparing the different homilies they had heard on the same readings from Holy Scripture. Today, we probably hold our denominational identities more lightly, so it is more common for couples to seek a church where they can worship, grow, and serve together, even across the Catholic–Protestant divide.

I encourage couples who are both Christian to seek a faith community that they can share. This may reflect my outlook as an Episcopalian, since Protestant and Catholic Christians will both find familiar elements in our worship life and theology. If you have time to undertake such a search before you sit down to plan your wedding, you will have a head start on resolving many of your wedding questions *and* you may find that your marriage is strengthened by practicing your religion in a setting that reminds you week by week of the vows you have made.

Clergy of different Christian traditions vary widely in their ability and willingness to participate in weddings outside their own church. Feel free to ask. But before you do, try to clarify in your own mind what it is you are asking for. Is the intention to acknowledge your heritage—or to have your marriage somehow validated by both traditions? Unfortunately, the openness to other expressions of Christian faith which began in the Roman Catholic Church with Vatican II has been somewhat diminished. Catholic clergy at the local level tend to be hamstrung by the hierarchy and overwhelmingly busy. Still, you can ask about how they might be able to participate. Catholic priests who are members of religious orders may have more flexibility than those who answer to a local congregation and bishop. Catholic clergy and religious who are family friends may be more comfortable participating in the service as guests than leaders. Asking them to lead a prayer at the reception or rehearsal dinner may be a good way to acknowledge their love and presence.

In one of my previous parishes, the priest at the neighboring Catholic church regularly told people that he did not regard people who were married in the Episcopal Church to be living in sin. And he asked the bride and groom to invite him to the reception. The official invitation to guest clergy (even those of our own denomination) to participate in a wedding is always issued by the rector/pastor of the host parish, of course.

Marriages of couples who are Jewish and Christian are very common in the United States. Once again, couples who resolve the larger questions about how each will practice his or her faith in the future will find that many of the wedding questions get answered in the process. Waiting until a first child is born and then negotiating whether to have a baptism or a *bris* is probably the worst-case scenario. As to the wedding, I have found that a few rabbis of the Reformed tradition are willing to participate in a wedding in a church, and a few more in Christian weddings held in a neutral site. I have taken part in some weddings that attempted to blend elements of both traditions, with both a rabbi and a Christian minister contributing in different ways. These were well-intentioned efforts but difficult to negotiate and ultimately not very satisfying. This is a good time to mention again that Anglicans do not see people married in a civil ceremony as any less married than those who have been married in a church. One option for Jewish-Christian couples is to be married in a civil ceremony by a friendly judge or wedding commissioner, while inviting the families' rabbi and pastor each to participate by offering a prayer, or simply being guests.

Outside the Judeo-Christian religions, there seems to be more comfort with simply having double ceremonies. It would not be unusual for a Hindu-Christian couple to have a church wedding, then to have a Hindu wedding on a nearby weekend. Most clergy of my Anglican tradition would probably be open to this, but we would raise questions about what happens after the wedding. Will the Hindu partner come to worship with their Christian spouse? Would he or she be baptized? What about the children who may be coming? As a pastor, the question in my heart is always: "Will this couple's difference in faith simply mean that one or the other—or both—simply ceases to practice their religion?"

The fact that you believe your marriage commitment and your faith are connected is very significant. I think you will find that the effort you expend in figuring out how to celebrate your marriage in the church will be very worthwhile.